YOUR KNOWLEDGE HAS VALUE

Bibliographic information published by the German National Library:

The German National Library lists this publication in the National Bibliography; detailed bibliographic data are available on the Internet at http://dnb.dnb.de .

Imprint:

Copyright © 2017 GRIN Verlag
Print and binding: Books on Demand GmbH, Norderstedt Germany
ISBN: 9783668726383

This book at GRIN:

https://www.grin.com/document/429036

Alexander Esse

Pricing Interest Rate Risk Derivatives Using Binomial Trees with MATLAB

GRIN Verlag

GRIN - Your knowledge has value

Since its foundation in 1998, GRIN has specialized in publishing academic texts by students, college teachers and other academics as e-book and printed book. The website www.grin.com is an ideal platform for presenting term papers, final papers, scientific essays, dissertations and specialist books.

Visit us on the internet:

http://www.grin.com/

http://www.facebook.com/grincom

http://www.twitter.com/grin_com

Eberhard Karls Universität Tübingen

Pricing Interest Rate Risk Derivatives Using Binomial
Trees with MATLAB (including code)

Author:	Alexander Esse
Submission Date:	31.08.2017

Contents

1 Abstract

In this assignment we approximate Oldrich Vasicek's (1977) term structure model with a binomial approach and show that it is convenient to use a recombining binomial tree to value interest rate derivatives in the Vasicek model.

First, we illustrate that our applied binomial approximations converge to the dynamic continuous-time Vasicek model with an increasing number of time steps (subperiods). Furthermore, we apply the binomial approach to value a Discount Bond, Coupon Bond and a Futures Contract on both a Discount and Coupon Bond. The resulting approximations will be compared to the respective analytical solution, which we use as a benchmark.

Thirdly, we determine the fair value of both an European and American Call and Put on a Discount Bond and Coupon Bond, respectively. We demonstrate that our estimated binomial prices converge with an increasing number of time steps. Moreover, we analyze both the behaviour of a Sraddle on a Discount Bond and the Early Exercise Premium of the considered American Options as a function of spot interest rates.

We obtain all results shown in this report from the software *Matlab*. Hence, the submitted *m.files* should be taken as a reference for a better understanding of the calculation procedures described in this report (Relevant Code is depicted in the Appendices).

Furthermore, to reduce computational effort and required time to run our code we apply a joint calculation of specific approximations rather than run a code individually for each Task. This is mainly because some specific securities and interest rate derivatives require the same underlying and identical matrices of the interest rates and transition probabilities from the binomial trees for the approximation procedure. This approach is suitable because we apply the identical number of subperiods for specific Tasks and, thus, for the respective securities and or derivatives.

2 A Binomial Approximation of Vasicek's Term Structure Model

To price a contingent claim, we first need to specify the driving process of the respective underlying source of uncertainty. Hence, in our case of interest rate-contingent claims we need a dynamic model for the term strucuture of interest spot rates. In the following, we will apply Oldrich Vasicek (1977) dynamic model. In this model the spot interest rate $r(t)$ follows the so-called Ornstein-Uhlenbeck (or mean-reverting Wiener model[1]) process

$$dr(t) = \kappa(\mu - r(t))dt + \sigma dw(t) \qquad (1)$$

with the constant parameters κ (mean reversion factor) μ (long-run average of the interest rate) and σ (interest rate volatility). Basically κ reflects the adjustment speed of the interest rate towards μ. The speed of adjustment is greater for higher values of κ and vice versa. If $r > \mu$ then the drift is negative, and when $r < \mu$ is present, the drift is positive (Ritchken (1996), p.543).

For an interest rate at time t_0 $(r(0) = r_0)$, the spot interest rate at time T $(r(T))$ is normally distributed with mean (Vasicek (1977), p. 185)

$$E[r(t) \mid r_0] = \mu + (r_0 - \mu)e^{-\kappa(t-t_0)} \qquad (2)$$

and variance

$$Var[r(t) \mid r_0] = \frac{\sigma^2}{2\kappa}(1 - e^{-2\kappa(t-t_0)}). \qquad (3)$$

As the interest rates are normally distributed, we could obtain negative interest rates with this process. However, when $t_0 \to -\infty$, the distribution becomes stationary with $E[r(t)] = \mu$ and $Var[r(t)] = \sigma^2/2\kappa$. As a result, the probability that interest rates become negative is largely mitigated (Ritchken (1996), p. 543).

In the following, we want to approximate the term structure model of Vasicek (1977) with a binomial approach. First, we discretize the time to maturity $(T - t_0)$ into n subperiods with width

$$\Delta t = \frac{T - t_0}{n}. \qquad (4)$$

Over each time increment, the interest rate can either increase to a specific level or decrease to another one with step size

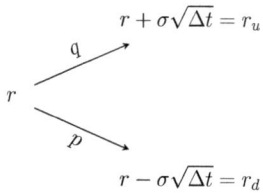

$$r + \sigma\sqrt{\Delta t} = r_u$$

$$r - \sigma\sqrt{\Delta t} = r_d$$

Figure 1: *Step Size of Interest Rate r.*

---

[1]see Ritchken (1996), p. 543.

As a result, we get a recombining binomial tree with the transition probability of an upward move (u)

$$q(r) = \frac{1}{2} + \frac{1}{2}\frac{\kappa(\mu - r)}{\sigma}\sqrt{\Delta t} \tag{5}$$

and the transition probability of a downward move (d)

$$p(r) = \frac{1}{2} - \frac{1}{2}\frac{\kappa(\mu - r)}{\sigma}\sqrt{\Delta t}. \tag{6}$$

Both probabilities depend on the state variable r, thus, they are not constant over time. Moreover, we settle the transition probabilities q and p to the interval $I = [0, \ldots, 1]$ if they end up out of I and, in turn, obtain censored probabilities. We compute the whole process in the function *'Binomial_Tree.m'* (see Binomial_Tree.m) in the lines 6-21 by typing *"'r, q, p'"* (as a mode-type) as an input-variable in our function in. This is helpful because we can access the same calculation-process for r, q and p with only one line in the master-file *'Assignment.m'* (see Assignment.m) through the mentioned function.

With Matlab we calculate r, q, p and all other approximations with a lower triangular matrix approach as depicted exemplary below:

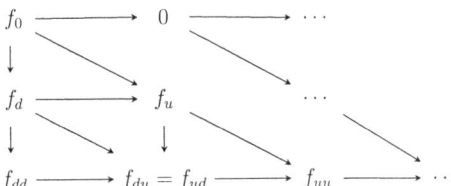

Figure 2: *Exemplary Matlab Binomial Tree.*

f is a generic value and represents the respective result for the individual nodes for all of our approximation values and matrices r, q, p and w examined here. In general, the upper diagonal in Figure (2) represents the pure up-moves and the left-handed vertical side the sole down-moves of the binomial tree. Each node is weighted with its respective transition probability q (see eq. (5)) or p (see eq. (6)). The dots illustrate the continued zero-values.

To obtain our approximations we use backward induction. We start at the expiration date T and determine the terminal values from the binomial tree for each state of the respective security. Subsequently, we value the respective price at each intermediate subperiod working backward in time until we reach t_0. Thus, the respective price at each node in time t is calculated as follows:

$$f_t = e^{-r_t \Delta t}(f_{t+\Delta t}^u \cdot q_{r_t} + f_{t+\Delta t}^d \cdot p_{r_t}). \tag{7}$$

However, for the approximation of the Futures Contract Value we do not discount the second term with $exp(-r_t \Delta t)$ in (7) to obtain the final estimation.

Hence, our initial point or the aproximation result for t_0 is always stored in the node (1,1). On the one hand, the matrix can become considerably large for increasing numbers of n and contains many zero-values, which are not relevant for our calculation of the approximations. This can increase the computational effort significantly. More than the higher accuracy we would obtain as n increases. On the other hand, this approach enables us to use the computational power of Matlab more efficiently because we do not need to start our binomial tree in the middle of the matrix, which would create an even bigger matrix.

To gain a recombining binomial tree of the spot interest rates called 'r' we use $n = 10$ subperiods and the following data:

r_0	μ	κ	T	t_0	σ
0.025	0.03	0.95	10	0	0.04

Table 1: *Parameter Values.*

In general, the parameter values are comprehensively relevant for all of our approximations.

The resulting matrix r contains both negative and positive interest spot rates. Overall, the lowest value is -37.50% and the highest is 42.50%.

We also determine the state-dependent transition probabilities q and p, and the total probability w to hit any point (j,k) of the binomial matrix in Matlab starting from t_0 (see for calculation process *Binomial_Tree.m*, Lines 40-48). To access the calculation of w in our function *Binomial_Tree.m* we need to type in "r, q, p, w" as a mode-type. The function then distinguishes the mode-type (Line 23) and leads us to the demanded calculation procedure and returns the matrices for r, q, p and w as output variables.

We observe for increasing values of n that the frequency distribution of the interest rate converges to a normal distribution at time T as depicted below in Figure (3).

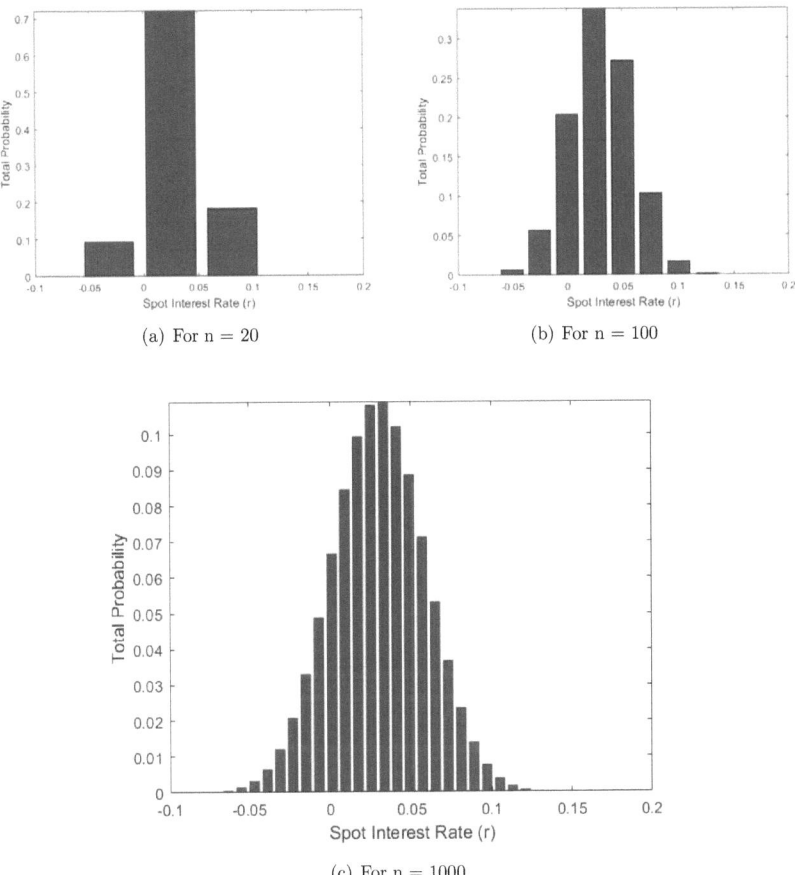

(a) For n = 20

(b) For n = 100

(c) For n = 1000

Figure 3: *Frequency Distribution at T of Interest Rate r.*

Therefore, we can show that for increasing values of n and, hence, diminishing Δt (see equation (eq.) (4)) the binomial procedure converges to the continous-time Vasicek model because the increments of the Ornstein-Uhlenbock process are normally distributed (Vasicek (1977), p. 185). This observation is also true when we compare the analytical solution for the expectation (eq. (2)) and variance (eq. (3)) of spot interest rates with our numerical approximations for varying numbers of subperiods. In total, our both approximations converge for higher values of n and coincide significantly already for $n = 100$, respectively, as Table (2) shows.

	n	10	20	100
Expectation	Approximation	0.0289	0.0301	0.03
	Exact Value	0.03	0.03	0.03
Variance	Approximation	0.000298347	0.000861661	0.000842105
	Exact Value	0.000842105	0.000842105	0.000842105

Table 2: Numerical Approximation: Expectation and Variance.

3 Valuation of Bonds and Derivatives

3.1 Part I

In this section, we first approximate the closed-form solution for a Discount Bond, Coupon Bond, both Forwards and Futures on Discount Bond, as well as Futures on Coupon Bonds. Subsequently, we approximate the fair value of both European Call and Put Options on Discount Bonds and of a Straddle on a Discount Bond. We obtain all approximations with a binomial approach as outlined in chapter 2.

Our analytical solution for a Discount Bond is provided by Vasicek (1977), pp. 185,186:

$$D(r, t, T) = exp(-A(t, T) \cdot r(t) - B(t, T)) \tag{8}$$

$$A(t, T) = \frac{1}{\kappa}(1 - e^{-\kappa(T-t)}) \tag{9}$$

$$B(t, T) = -A(t, T) \cdot R + (T - t) \cdot R + \frac{\sigma^2}{4\kappa^3}(1 - e^{-\kappa(T-t)})^2 \tag{10}$$

$$\tag{11}$$

with

$$R = \mu - \frac{\sigma^2}{2\kappa^2}. \tag{12}$$

Closed-form solution (11) is implemented in the Matlab-function "$D.m$". We also use the provided functions from class to obtain analytical solutions for the residual securities such as $B.m$ for a Coupon Bond, $G.m$ for a Forward on Discount Bonds and $H.m$ for Futures on Discount Bonds (as the mentioned functions were already given, codes are not depicted).

We implemented all required binomial pricing procedures in the function "$Binomial\_Price.m$" (see Binomial_Price.m). To access the individual approach we type in one of our defined types, e.g. "$DiscountBond$" for the approximation procedure of a Discount

6

Bond, and the function accesses the respective calculations. In general, for the binomial approximation, we first predefine the size of the binomial matrix and the terminal values for each state of the respective security in dependence on parameter n (see *Binomial_Price.m*, Lines 11,12 as an example for a Discount Bond). Thereupon the backward induction process follows as described above in chapter 2. The resulting matrix or matrices are the output variables ($'Bin1'$, $'Bin2'$) of our Matlab-function.

Moreover, in the case of a Coupon Bond we additionally need to specify the coupon payment dates in dependence of the number of chosen subperiods. Therefore we check in "*Binomial_Price.m*" for every row j if the payment date is due with a combined if-condition (see Line 64). We use for this purpose the implemented Matlab-function "$mod(\bullet)$". For every coupon-payment date-row j the mod-function returns the value 1 (for instance if $n = 120$ and $T = 12$ we get for the first coupon-payment date $mod(11, (120/12)) = 1$) and we add the cash-flow amount of the considered coupon to the Coupon Bond value in the respective nodes (see Line 65). Otherwise, the mod-function returns a value greater or smaller one. In order to prevent that we add a coupon if $n = 1$ ($mod(1, (120/12)) = 1$), and thus in t_0, we additionally review if the row-number of j is greater than 1 (see for whole loop-structure *Binomial_Price.m*, Lines 61-70). We want to stress that this approach returns appropriate approximation values only for $n \geq 120$ and simultaneously n-values which are multiples of 12, such as $n = [120, 360, 2400, 3600]$.

Furthermore, we need to define for the Futures Contract and the considered Options the exact row-line j, in which the respective security terminates for $T_{Security} < T_{Underlying}$ or $T < T_U$.
Hence, we calculate

$$cc = \frac{T - t_0}{T_U - t_0} \cdot n \tag{13}$$

which gives us the exact row-line in which the security terminates during the time to maturity of the underlying in dependence of n. For the case of $T = 2.5$ and $T_U = 10$ the number of subperiods must be a multiple of 4 to obtain an integer for cc, which is essential for Matlab and for not biased results. If elsewise $T_U = 12$ is present, n needs to be a multiple of $(5/24)$.

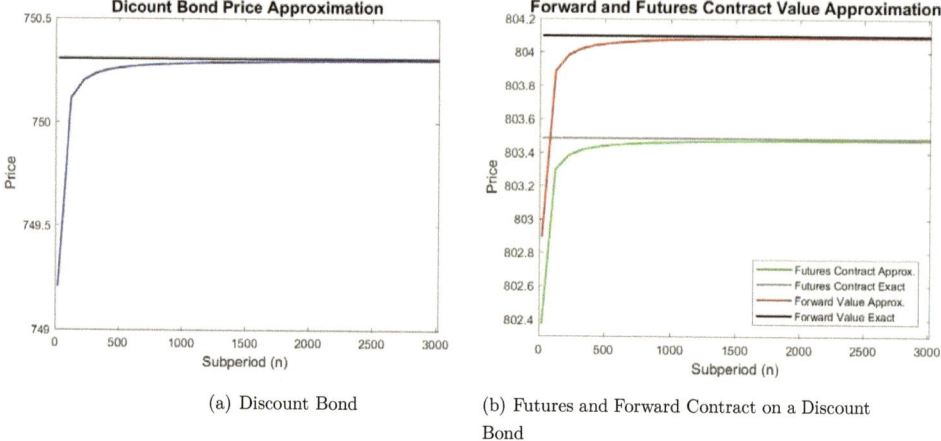

(a) Discount Bond

(b) Futures and Forward Contract on a Discount Bond

Figure 4: *Binomial Approximation for increasing n.*

Figure (4) illustrates our approximation results for a Discount Bond (4(a)) and both a Futures and Forward Contract on a Discount Bond (4(b)). The analytical solution for the Discount Bond with $T = 10$ and a face value $F = 1000$ is "D_Exact" = 750.3073. We obtain for the Futures Contract "H_Exact" = 803.4832 and for the Forward "G_Exact" = 804.0997. Both contracts are written on the considered Discount Bond and have a time to maturity of $T = 2.5$ years.

We observe that the approximation of all three securities approaches from below to the analytical price and distinctly deviates from it for $n < 1000$. However, for $n \geq 1000$ all considered approximations in Figure (4) clearly converge to the closed-form solution. For instance, the absolute deviation of our Discount Bond price estimation ("D_Approx" = 750.2993') to the exact value is 0.008 with $n = 3020$. The respective differences to the closed-form solution of our Futures Contract ("H_Approx" = 803.4755) is 0.0077 and of the Forward ("G_Approx" = 804.0909) 0.0088.

The fair value of a Coupon Bond with $T = 12$, face value $F = 60000$, a coupon rate of $c = 3.0\%$ and a constant interest rate $r = r_0 = 0.025$ is $B = 62304.0633$. The Bond's price is above par because its fixed coupon rate exceeds the prevailing market rate (r_0).

8

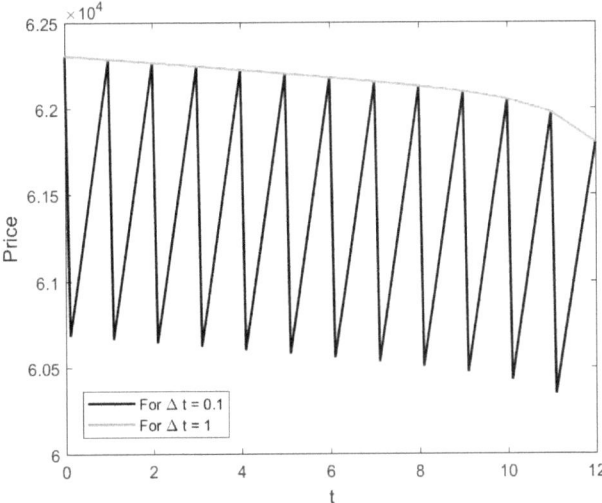

Figure 5: *Coupon Bond Price Evolution over remaining 12 Years until Expiration.*

Figure (5) shows that the Coupon Bond price decreases continously as time moves towards its expiration $(t \to 12)$ for a constant interest rate $(r = r_0)$. For $t > 10$ the negative slope of the price increases. Eventually the Bond's price reaches the amount of its face value plus terminal coupon payment - resulting in "B" $= 61800$ for $T - t = 0$.

If we choose a time step of $\Delta t = 1$, the graph tends to indicate a smooth price evolution during its remaining time to maturity. However, if we choose a smaller time step $(\Delta t = 0.1)$, the price evolution appears more sawtooth-shaped. This is due to the accrued interest, which builds until a coupon payment is made. Then the value drops by the coupon amount that was disbursed. Hence, the green line in Figure (5) represents the pure dirty price. A connection of the lower ends of the black line would illustrate the clean price of the bond and the difference between both line graphs would be the amount of accrued interest.

The approximated fair value of the given Futures Contract $(T = 2.5)$ from Task 3.3.4 on the Coupon Bond examined above for $n = 3600$ is "$H\_CouponBond\_Approx$" $= 61091.2568$.

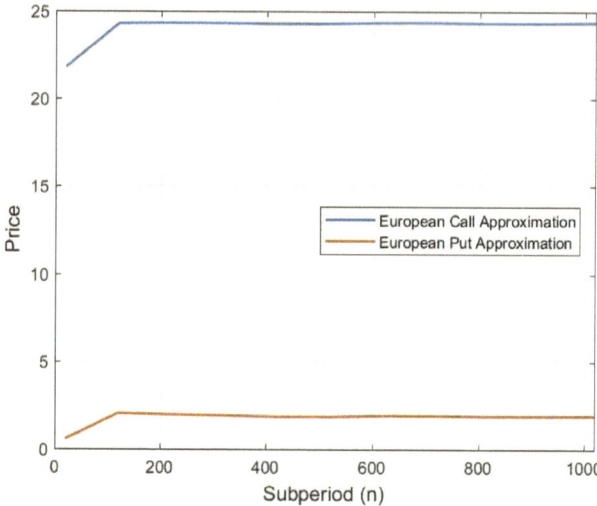

Figure 6: *European Call and Put Price Approximation for varying Subperiods.*

In Figure (6) we see that the approximations for both the European Call and Put Option on a Discount Bond converge with increasing n. We obtain with $n = 1020$ an estimated fair value for the Call of "$Call\_European\_DB\_Approx$" = 24.3512 and for the Put "$Put\_European\_DB\_Approx$" = 1.8885.

To examine whether the Put-Call-Parity holds, we replicate the Call price for a Call Option on a Discount Bond with

$$Call_{Parity}^{DB} = Put_{E,Approx}^{DB} + D_U \cdot F - D \cdot K \qquad (14)$$

and a Call Option on a Coupon Bond with

$$Call_{Parity}^{CB} = Put_{E,Approx}^{CB} + B - D \cdot K - PV(C). \qquad (15)$$

DB stands for "Discount Bond", CB for "Coupon Bond" and E for "European". $Put_{E,Approx}^{DB}$ is our approximated European Put price on a Discount Bond or, respectively, Coupon Bond if $Put_{E,Approx}^{CB}$. F represents the Face Value, K is the strike price of the Option, while D_U is the current value of the underlying Discount Bond with $F = 1$ and $T_U = 10$. D is the price of a corresponding Discount Bond with $T = 2.5$. B represents the fair value of a Coupon Bond with $T_U = 12$, while $PV(C)$ is the total present value of the coupon payments to be paid out over the remaining life $(T - t_0)$ of the option. We calculate the Discount Bond price with the given Matlab-function $D.m$ and the Coupon Bond price with $B.m$.

We implement formula (14) in our *for-loop* for the binomial approximation of the

Options from 3.3.5 (see *Assignment_5.m*, Lines 216-240) to see if the Put-Call-Parity and the Call Price approximation converge for increasing subperiods. Because the second term in Formula (14) - after the Put price estimation - is constant, we calculate it outside of the *for-loop* mentioned above and store the result in the variable *Residual_Parity_DB* (see Line 195). This leads to less needed computational effort because we do not compute the same result for every loop-pass depending on n. Subsequently, we add this variable within every predetermined loop-pass to the Put price estimation (see Line 239) and store the results in the vector "*Call_Parity_DB_Graph*".

Subperiods	20	520	1020
European Call Approximation	21.7810	24.2866	24.3512
Put-Call-Parity: Call Price	23.0332	24.3353	24.3760
Absolute Difference	1.25221	0.04871	0.02482

Table 3: *Convergence of Put-Call-Parity for European Call on a Discount Bond.*

Table (3) illustrates that the Put-Call-Parity is valid for the considered options on the Discount Bond and the accuracy of the approximation significantly increases for higher values of n.

The binomial approximation of the fair value of a corresponding Straddle (European Call + Put Price) expiring in $T = 2.5$ years with the underlying Discount Bond from above for $n = 1020$ is depicted below in Table (4).

σ	r	Fair Value
0.0400	0.0250	26.2397
0.0710	0.0250	42.4166

Table 4: *Binomial Approximation of Straddle Fair Value on a Discount Bond.*

We observe that the Straddle-value, ceteris paribus, distinctly raises for increasing spot interest rate's volatility. This is mainly because the price of both Call and Put Options on Bonds - alike Options on underlying stocks - basically increase due to the higher underlying risk and, hence, stronger fluctuation of the underlying's price evolution.

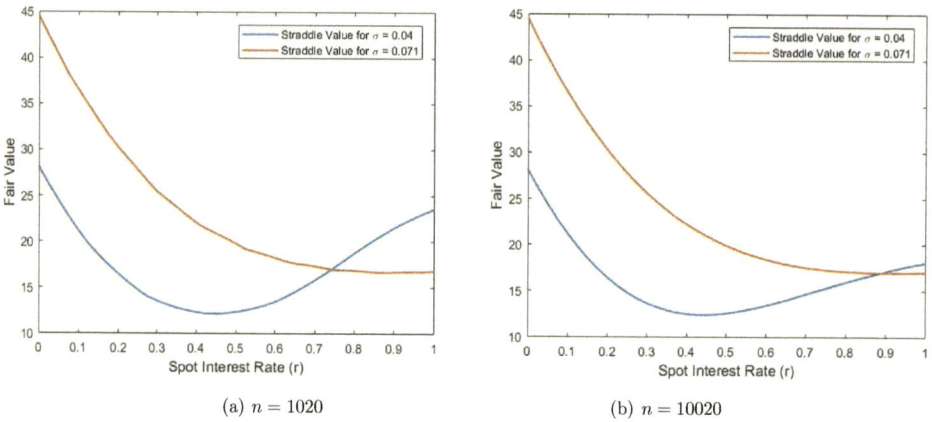

(a) $n = 1020$ (b) $n = 10020$

Figure 7: *Binomial Approximation Fair Value Sraddle on a Discount Bond.*

Figure (7) shows the price evolution of an European Straddle on a Discount Bond as a function of r_0. In general, it illustrates the higher value of a Straddle for higher volatility and $r_0 < 0.75$. In Figure (7(a)) it appears that the Sraddle-value for $\sigma = 0.04$ would significantly exceed the corresponding price for $\sigma = 0.071$ if $r > 0.75$. However, as we raise the number of subperiods to $n = 10020$, we observe that this difference clearly reduces but still remains for $r > 0.90$.

We want to emphasize that our following analysis and interpretation of the results is based on calculations for $n = 10020$ subperiods. However, we calculated the corresponding graphs in Figure (8) separately because it would take too much computational time to run the calculations as a whole code for this assignment for so many time steps in Task 3.3.6. Therefore, we have left the relevant line 201 in *Assignment_5.m* commented with "%" but compare in the following both results (for $n = 1020$ and $n = 10020$). We have chosen such a high value for n because we observed that the results change significantly as we increase the number of subperiods and wanted to avoid biased approximations shown in the graphs.

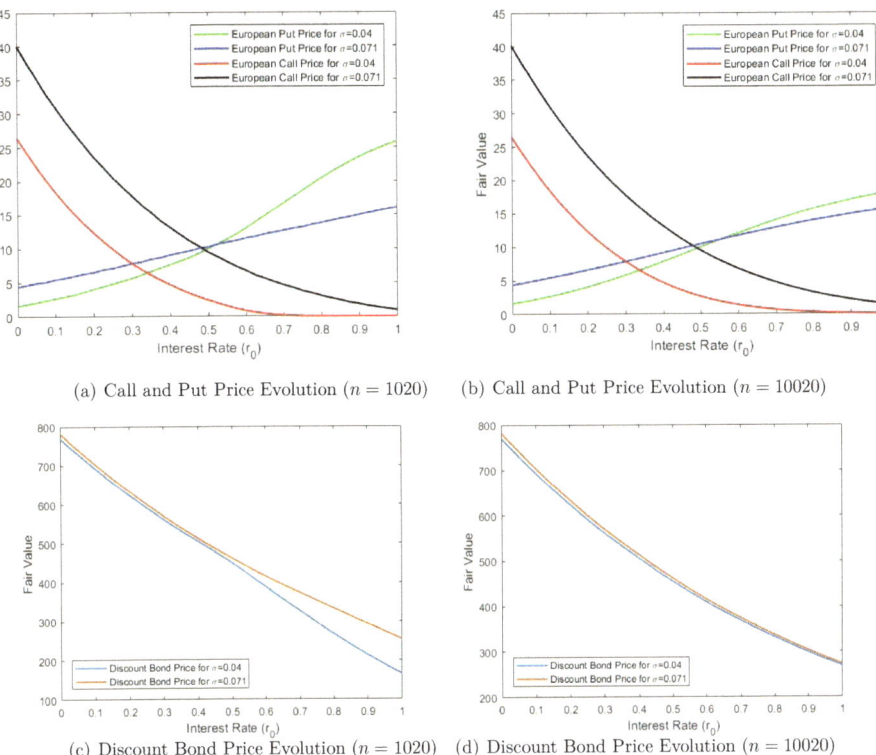

(a) Call and Put Price Evolution ($n = 1020$) (b) Call and Put Price Evolution ($n = 10020$)

(c) Discount Bond Price Evolution ($n = 1020$) (d) Discount Bond Price Evolution ($n = 10020$)

Figure 8: *Binomial Approximation: Discount Bond, European Call and Put for varying r_0.*

We observe a distinct difference in the Discount Bond price approximation for $\sigma = 0.04$ and $r_0 > 0.50$, and thus, in the price evolution of the European Put on the same Bond. Basically, the Put Option's price reacts more sensitive for increasing r_0. All residual approximations are not strongly affected by the increase of subperiods regarding changes in the direction of their price development. The strong surge of the Put price for low volatility is the predominant driving factor for the significant difference of the Straddle value in Figure (7) for $\sigma = 0.04$, when we compare Subfigure (7(a)) with (7(b)).

Basically, as the interest rate increases, the Discount Bond Price diminishes (see (8(d))) and, as a result, the value of the Call, as well. The falling Bond price, however, leads to a rising Put price. Since the Call price is higher than the Put price for low interest spot rates, relative losses of the former have a more severe impact on the Straddle value, which, in turn, generally falls for increasing r_0 (see (7)). For $\sigma - 0.071$ (high volatility case) this effect is balanced for $r_0 > 0.70$ and remains on a level around the value 17 for $n = 10020$. In the case of $\sigma = 0.04$ (low volatility case) the Straddle value starts to increase for $r_0 \geq 0.40$. This is mainly because the Put price raises more strongly than the corresponding Call price and exceeds its price at $r_0 = 0.3250$ in the low volatility case (in the high volatility case at $r_0 = 0.50$). Moreover, the Put price (for low volatility) exceeds the Put value from the high volatility case over time and crosses it at $r_0 = 0.5750$ due to the continously lower Discount Bond price for lower volatility (see Subfigure (8(d))). Furthermore, the lower interest rate volatility leads to the fact that the transition probability of an upward move – if $\sigma = 0.04$ – occurs relatively later than for the high volatility case for increasing r_0 when we compare the q-matrices for both volatility cases. Moreover, this leads to the fact that the first probability for an upward move emerges significantly later too, as $r_0 \to 100\%$. Hence, the overall probability for increasing Bond prices declines faster than for $\sigma = 0.071$, which is more beneficial for the Put price. This makes the given Put Option in the case of $\sigma = 0.04$ more valuable than in the case of high volatility. Therefore, the Straddle value increases over time for $\sigma = 0.04$, and eventually exceeds the Straddle value in the high volatility case.

3.2   Part II

In the following we determine the fair value of both an European Call and Put on a Coupon Bond with the binomial approach as described in chapter (2). Furthermore, we approximate the fair value of American Call and Put Options on both a Discount Bond and on a Coupon Bond.
We use for the estimation of the price of an American-style option formula (7) and additionally examine whether the price in the respective node or the value of an immediate exercise of the option is more valuable. Therefore we calculate

$$Call_t^{Am} = max(f_t, D_t^{Bin} - K) \tag{16}$$

for an American (Am) Call Option and

$$Put_t^{Am} = max(f_t, K - D_t^{Bin}) \tag{17}$$

for an American Put Option. K is the strike price and D_t^{Bin} represents the binomial Discount Bond price at time t. For an American Option on a Coupon Bond we take B_t^{Bin} - the respective binomial Coupon Bond price. To obtain the fair value of the respective option we also use backward induction as described above.
The fair value of an American Call and Put with $T = 2.5$ years and $K = 780$ on a Discount Bond with face value $F = 1000$ and time to maturity of $T_U = 10$ years is "$Call\_American\_DB\_Approx$" = 25.5072 and "$Put\_American\_DB\_Approx$" = 29.8864 for $n = 1020$.

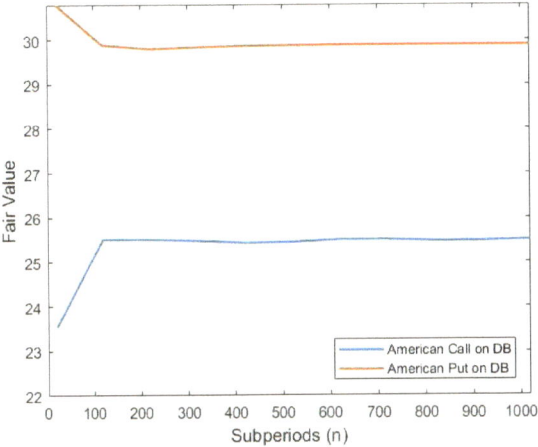

Figure 9: *Approximated American Call and Put Price on a Discount Bond.*

Figure (9) illustrates that our price approximations converge with increasing n. However, we already achieve for $n \geq 150$ estimators, which are sufficiently close to the convergence level.

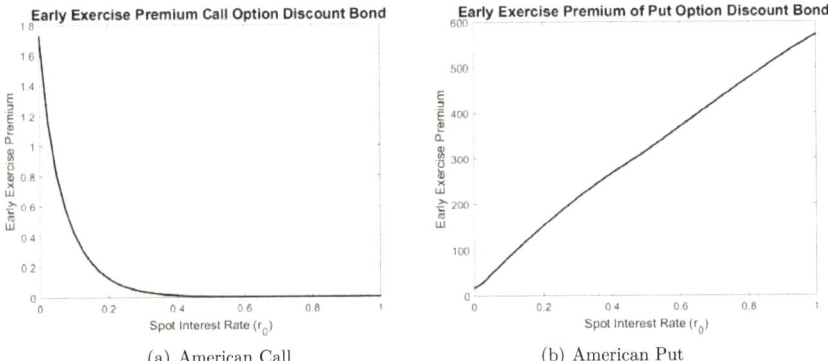

(a) American Call

(b) American Put

Figure 10: *Early Exercise Premium: American Options on Discount Bond.*

The early exercise premium (EEP) is the difference between the considered American Call or Put Option on a Discount Bond and its corresponding European counterpart examined above (see Figure (6)). The EEP of the American Call Option decreases significantly for higher interest rates. This is mainly because the price of a Discount Bond declines for increasing interest rates, which leads automatically to a lower price of both an European and American Call. Moreover, the likelihood for further declining bond prices increases as well, which makes the American Call less valuable to hold and, as a result, the early exercise premium diminishes. In Figure (10(a)) the early exercise premium reduces to values close to zero for $r_0 \geq 0.40$.

The EEP of an American Put Option, on the other hand, rises distinctly for increasing spot interest rates. This is mainly because the possibility for decreasing Bond prices increases. In such situation, the possibility to exercise the Option and, thus, to sell the Discount Bond for $K > D_t$ at any time becomes more valuable for the option-holder. That, in turn, leads to a higher value of an American Put Option compared to the European counterpart.

Subperiods	1200	3600
Ep. Call	2227.6400	2228.4188
Ep. Put	76.4120	75.9822
Am. Call	3663.7180	3660.5277
Am. Put	359.8575	363.1621

Table 5: *European and American Options on a Coupon Bond for varying subperiods (n) and $r_0 = 0.025$.*

The approximated fair values of an European (Ep.) Call and Put ($T = 2.5$, $K = 58800$) on a Coupon Bond with $F = 60000$, coupon rate $c = 0.03$ and time to maturity $T_U = 12$ are "Ep.Call" $= 2228.4188$ (in Matlab: "Call_European_CB_Approx") and "Ep.Put" $= 75.9822$ (in Matlab: "Put_European_CB_Approx") (see Table (5) for $n = 3600$).

However, in this case, the Put-Call-Parity (PCP) is not valid because the replicated Call price from the PCP is "Call_Parity_CB" $= 3217.2698$ (for $n = 3600$), which clearly deviates from our approximation result. As for the Put-Call-Parity on a Discount Bond, we calculate the constant part (sum except Put Price estimator) of the replication formula for the Call Option on a Coupon Bond (eq. (15)) outside of the $for-loop$ (see "Assignmnet_5.m", Lines 391-392) and add it to the calculation of the demanded result within the loop for every step of the loop-procedure (see Line 424).

Our approximated fair values of an American (Am.) Call and Put both with $T = 2.5$ and $K = 58800$ on the same Coupon Bond as mentioned above are "Am.Call" $= 3660.5277$ (in Matlab: "Call_American_CB_Approx") and "Am.Put" $= 363.1621$ (in Matlab: "Put_American_CB_Approx") for $n = 3600$.

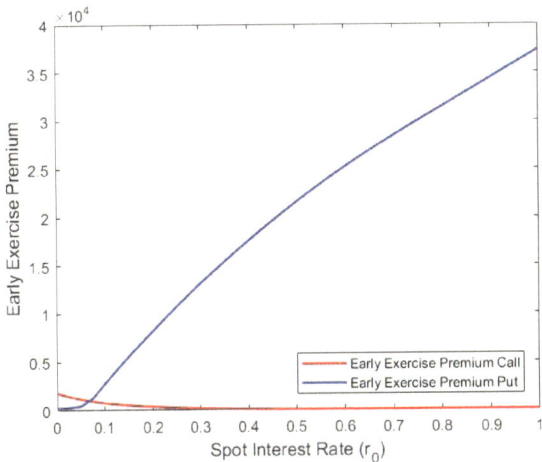

Figure 11: *Early Exercise Premium: American Options on Coupon Bond.*

The Early Exercise Premium (EEP) of the American Call Option is for $r_0 = [0, ..., 1]$ relatively small and declines for increasing spot interest rates. This is mainly because a Coupon Bond's price diminishes for increasing interest rates, which, in fact, basically makes a Call Option less valuable. The probability for increasing Bond prices reduces simultaneously, as well. Therefore, an American-style option becomes less beneficial and its price approaches the price of an European Call Option. Hence, the EEP decreases.

The American Put Option's EEP increases slowly for $r_0 \leq 0.05$. However, for $r_0 > 0.05$ the Early Exercise Price leaps for increasing spot interest rates. This is due to the rising likelihood of falling Bond prices and, thus, to benefit from selling the Coupon Bond at any time for $(t_0 < T)$ in order to benefit from the higher interest market rate r_0. As a result, the American-style Put Option becomes significantly more valuable than an European one, which, in turn, increases the EEP strongly.

4   Conclusion

We illustrate in this assignment that using recombining binomial trees is suitable to value complex interest rate derivates in the Vasicek model. In general, our approximations converge to the continuous-time Vasicek model and to its analytical solutions for a Discount Bond, expectation and the variance of interest rates. Moreover, our estimated prices for Call and Put Options on both Discount Bonds and Coupon Bonds converge to a certain level for increasing subperiods. This holds for

European- style as well as for American-style options.

The Early Exercise Premium of a Call Option on both Discount and Coupon Bonds as a function of interest rates decreases for rising market rates. The corresponding Put Option's premium, however, increases for increasing interest rates. Furthermore, an European Put on a Discount Bond reacts more sensitive for higher volatility and exceeds a respective Put price for lower lower volatility if $r_0 > 0.50$. As a result, a Straddle consisting of an European Call and Put both on a Discount Bond also exceeds for lower fluctuation of interest rates its corresponding price (for higher volatility) over time.

Appendices

Assignment.m

```
1   tic;
2   %% Given Parameter Values %%
3   clear; clc;
4
5   r0 = 0.025;      mu = 0.03;       kp = 0.95;
6   T = 10;          t0 = 0;          sg = 0.04;
7
8   %% 3.1      << Binomial Tree of the Spot Interest Rate >>
9   n = 10;
10  % ----- We additionally determine the transition probabilities q and p ----- %
11  [r,q,p] = Binomial_Tree('r,q,p',n,t0,T,r0,sg,mu,kp);
12
13  %% 3.2      << Expectation, Variance and Histogram >>
14  nl = [10,20,100,1000];
15
16  %%%% Preallocation of Vectors %%%%
17  Er_Approx_Graph = nan(1,length(nl));
18  Var_Approx_Graph = nan(1,length(nl));
19
20  for kk=1:1:length(nl)       % Referring to each of the predefined values of nl in Line 20
21      n=nl(kk);
22      [r_Hist,~,~,w] = Binomial_Tree('r,q,p,w',n,t0,T,r0,sg,mu,kp);
23
24      %%%% Approximation Values %%%%
25      Er_Approx = r_Hist(n+1,:)*w(n+1,:)';
26      Var_Approx = (r_Hist(n+1,:)-Er_Approx).^2*w(n+1,:)';
27      Er_Approx_Graph(1,kk) = Er_Approx;
28      Var_Approx_Graph(1,kk) = Var_Approx;
29
30      %%%% Plotting %%%%
31      % ----- Frequency Distribution at T for predetermined Values of n = nl (see Line 21) ----- %
32      figure(kk);     % <<<< Figure 3 in Report >>>>
33      bar(r_Hist(n+1,:),w(n+1,:));
34      axis([-0.1 0.2 0.0 inf])
35      title('Frequency Distribution at T','FontSize',14,'FontWeight','bold')
36      xlabel('Spot Interest Rate (r)','FontSize',12);
37      ylabel('Total Probability','FontSize',12);
38  end
39
40  %%%% Closed-Form Solutions by Vasicek (1977) %%%%
41  Er_Exact=mu+(r0-mu).*exp(-kp.*(T-t0));          % Formula (25) [Vasicek (1977), p. 185] for
        t0 <= T
42  Var_Exact=sg^2.*(1-exp(-2.*kp.*(T-t0)))./(2.*kp);   % Formula (26) [Vasicek (1977), p. 185] for
        t0 <= T
43
44  %% 3.3      << Valuation of Bonds and Derivatives PART I >>
45  %% 3.3.1    << Valuation Discount Bond >>
46  %% 3.3.2    << Valuation Futures Contract on Discount Bond >>
47  F = 1000;                                       % Predetermined Face Value
```

```matlab
48   T_Future = 2.5;                                  % Time−to−Maturity of Futures Contract
49   n2 = 20:100:3020;                                % Number of Time−Steps
50
51   %%%% Preallocation the Vector for the Approximation Values for varying Values for n %%%%
52   % For Discount Bond Value Approximation %
53   D_Bin_Graph = nan(1,length(n2));                 % For Discount Bond Value Approximation
54   D_Bin_Graph_F = D_Bin_Graph;                     % Relevant for Approximation of Forward Price
55   H_Bin_Graph = nan(1,length(n2));                 % For Futures Contract Value Approximation
56   G_Bin_Graph = nan(1,length(n2));                 % For Forward Value Approximation
57
58   %%%% Binomial Grid %%%%
59   for ii = 1:1:length(n2)
60       n = n2(ii);
61
62       %%%% Binomial Grid for r,q and p %%%%
63       [r_DB,q_DB,p_DB] = Binomial_Tree('r,q,p',n,t0,T,r0,sg,mu,kp);
64       % −−−−− Time to Maturity of Forward Contract corresponds with one of Futures Contract −−−−− %
65       [r_F,q_F,p_F] = Binomial_Tree('r,q,p',n,t0,T_Future,r0,sg,mu,kp);
66
67       %%%% Binomial Grid for Discount Bond %%%%
68       % −−−−− For 3.3.1 and 3.3.2 −−−−− %
69       cc=((T_Future−t0)/(T−t0))*n;                 % Obtaining the Column Number at which the Futures
                 Contract expires
70
71       [D_Bin,H_Bin] = Binomial_Price(n,t0,T,r_DB,q_DB,p_DB,F,'Futures Contract Discount Bond',cc);
72       [D_Bin_F] = Binomial_Price(n,t0,T_Future,r_F,q_F,p_F,F,'Discount Bond');
73
74       %%%% Storing Approximation Values %%%%
75       % −−−−− For 3.3.1 −−−−− %       << Approximation of Discount Bond with F = 1000 %
76       D_Bin_Graph(ii) = D_Bin(1,1);
77       % −−−−− For 3.3.2 −−−−− %       << Approximation of Futures Contract and Forward Contract on
                 Discount Bond >>
78       H_Bin_Graph(ii) = H_Bin(1,1);
79       D_Bin_Graph_F(ii) = D_Bin_F(1,1);
80       G_Bin_Graph(ii) = (D_Bin_Graph(1,ii)/D_Bin_Graph_F(1,ii)).*F;
81   end
82
83   %%%% Binomial Approximation Values for 3.3.1 and 3.3.2 %%%%
84   D_Approx = D_Bin_Graph(ii−1);
85   H_Approx = H_Bin_Graph(ii−1);
86   G_Approx = G_Bin_Graph(ii−1);
87
88   %%%% Closed−Form Solutions %%%%
89   % We have to multiply all Formulas with F in order to get the Price of a Bond with Face Value F
         = 1000 %
90   D_Exact = D(t0,T,r0,mu,sg,kp)*F;                 % Closed−Form Solution for a Discount Bond with
                 Face Value F
91   H_Exact = H(t0,T_Future,T,r0,mu,sg,kp)*F;        % Closed−Form Solution for a Futures Contract on
                 a Discount Bond
92   G_Exact = G(t0,T_Future,T,r0,mu,sg,kp)*F;        % Closed−Form Solution for a Forward Contract on
                 a Discount Bond
93
94   %−−−−−−−−−−−−−−−−−−−−−−−−−−−−−−−−−−−−−−−−−−−−−−−−−−−−−−−−−−−−−−−−−−−−−−−−−−−−−−−−−−−−−−−−−−%
95   %%%% Plotting %%%%
96   % −−−−− Approximation to the respective Closed−form Solution for increasing n −−−−− %
97   % −−−−− For 3.3.1 −−−−− %
98   kk = kk+1;
99   figure(kk);        % <<<< Figure 4(a) in Report >>>>
100  plot(n2,D_Bin_Graph,'b','LineWidth',1.5);
101  hold on
102  plot(n2,D_Exact*ones(1,length(n2)),'k','LineWidth',1.5);
103  axis([0 3020 749 750.5])
104  title('Dicount Bond Price Approximation','FontSize',14,'FontWeight','bold')
105  xlabel('Subperiod (n)','FontSize',12);
106  ylabel('Price','FontSize',12);
107  hold off
108  saveas(gcf,'3.3.1_Approx_DiscountBond.jpg');
109
110  % −−−−− For 3.3.2 −−−−− %
111  kk = kk+1;
112  figure(kk)        % <<<< Figure 4(b) in Report >>>>
113  Graph_Combined = [H_Bin_Graph;H_Exact*ones(1,length(n2));G_Bin_Graph;G_Exact*ones(1,length(n2))
                 ];
114  p = plot(n2,Graph_Combined,'LineWidth',1.5);
115  % Specifies the respective Color of the Rows from the Matrix' Graph_Combined' %
116  set(p,{'color'},num2cell([0,0.7,0;0.5,0.5,0.5;1,0,0;0,0,0],2));
117  axis([0 3020 802.3 804.2])
118  title('Forward and Futures Contract Value Approximation','FontSize',14,'FontWeight','bold')
119  xlabel('Subperiod (n)','FontSize',12);
120  ylabel('Price','FontSize',12);
121  legend({'Futures Contract Approx.','Futures Contract Exact','Forward Value Approx.',...
122          'Forward Value Exact'},'Location','southeast')
```

19

```matlab
123    saveas(gcf,'3.3.2_Approx_FuturesForwardContract_DiscountBond.jpg');
124
125    %% 3.3.3      << Valuation of a Coupon Bond >>
126    T_Coupon = 12;
127    F_Coupon_Bond = 60000;
128    c = 0.03;
129    Coupon = c*F_Coupon_Bond;
130    t = T_Coupon:-0.1:t0;
131    t1 = T_Coupon:-1:t0;
132
133    %%%% Preallocation of Matrices %%%%
134    B_Exact = nan(1,length(t));              % Coupon Bond Vector for time step Delta t = 0.1
135    B_Exact1 = nan(1,length(t1));            % Coupon Bond Vector for time step Delta t = 1
136
137    % ----- For Delta t = 1 ----- %
138    for tt = 1:1:length(t1)
139        B_Exact1(tt) = B(t1(tt),T_Coupon,Coupon,F_Coupon_Bond,r0,mu,sg,kp);
140    end
141    % ----- For Delta t = 0.1 ----- %
142    for tt = 1:1:length(t)
143        B_Exact(tt) = B(t(tt),T_Coupon,Coupon,F_Coupon_Bond,r0,mu,sg,kp);
144    end
145    % Coupon Bond Price with remaining Time to Maturity of 12 Years %
146    B = B_Exact(length(t));
147
148    %
_____%

149    %%%% Plotting %%%%
150    % ----- Coupon Bond Price Evolution over the remaining 12 Years ----- %
151    kk = kk+1;
152    figure(kk)         % <<<< Figure 5 in Report >>>>
153    plot(t,B_Exact,'k','LineWidth',1.5);
154    hold on
155    plot(t1,B_Exact1,'g','LineWidth',1.5)
156    grid on
157    title('Coupon Bond Price Evolution','FontSize',14,'FontWeight','bold')
158    xlabel('t','FontSize',12);
159    ylabel('Price','FontSize',12);
160    legend({'For \Delta t = 0.1','For \Delta t = 1'}...
161                      ,'Location','southwest')
162    hold off
163    saveas(gcf,'3.3.3_CouponBond.jpg');
164    %% 3.3.4      << Valuation of a Futures Contract on a Coupon Bond >>
165    n_Coupon = [120,360,1200,3600];
166
167    %%%% Preallocation of Matrices %%%%
168    H_CouponBond_Bin_Graph = nan(1,length(n_Coupon));
169
170    for ii = 1:1:length(n_Coupon)
171        n = n_Coupon(ii);
172
173        %%%% Binomial Grid for r,q and p %%%%
174        [r_Coupon,q_Coupon,p_Coupon] = Binomial_Tree('r,q,p',n,t0,T_Coupon,r0,sg,mu,kp);
175
176        %%%% Binomial Grid for Futures Contract on Coupon Bond %%%%
177        cc = ((T_Future-t0)/(T_Coupon-t0))*n;     % Obtaining the Column Number where the Futures
                   Contract expires %
178
179        [H_CouponBond_Bin] = Binomial_Price(n,t0,T_Coupon,r_Coupon,q_Coupon,p_Coupon,...
180                            F_Coupon_Bond,'Futures Contract Coupon Bond',c,cc);
181        H_CouponBond_Bin_Graph(ii) = H_CouponBond_Bin(1,1);
182    end
183
184    %%%% Binomial Approximation-Value of the Futures Contract %%%%
185    H_CouponBond_Approx = H_CouponBond_Bin_Graph(length(n_Coupon));
186
187    %% 3.3.5      << European Call and Put on a Discount Bond >>
188    %% 3.3.6      << Straddle on a Discount Bond >>
189    %% 3.4.2      << American Call and Put on a Discount Bond >>
190    T_Option = 2.5;          % Time to Maturity of both European Options
191    K = 0.78*F;              % Strike Price: Valid for Both European Options on Discount Bond
192    rr = 0:0.025:1;          % Vector of Interest Rates
193
194    % ----- For 3.3.5 ----- %
195    Residual_Parity_DB = D(t0,T,r0,mu,sg,kp)*F-D(t0,T_Option,r0,mu,sg,kp)*K;
196    % ----- For 3.3.6 ----- %
197    sg_loop = [0.04, 0.071];
198
199    n3 = 20:100:1020;
200    n4 = [820,1020];
201    % n4 = [10020];      % ----- For Additional Analysis ----- %
```

20

```matlab
202
203   %%%% Preallocation of Matrices and Vectors %%%%
204   % ——— For 3.3.5 and 3.3.6 ——— %                          << ——— For 3.4.2 ——— >>
205   Call_European_DB_Graph = nan(1,length(n3));               Call_American_DB_Graph = nan(1,length
          (n3));                                                     (n3));
206   Put_European_DB_Graph = nan(1,length(n3));                Put_American_DB_Graph = nan(1,length(
          n3));                                                      n3));
207   Straddle = nan(length(sg_loop),length(rr),length(n4));    Early_Exercise_Premium_Call_DB = nan
          (1,length(rr));                                           (1,length(rr));
208   Call_Parity_DB_Graph = nan(1,length(n3));                 Early_Exercise_Premium_Put_DB = nan
          (1,length(rr));                                           (1,length(rr));
209
210   % ——— For 3.3.6 Additional Analysis ——— %
211   D_Bin_Option_Graph1 = nan(length(sg_loop),length(rr),length(n4));
212   Call_Europ_DB_Graph1 = nan(length(sg_loop),length(rr),length(n4));
213   Put_Europ_DB_Graph1 = nan(length(sg_loop),length(rr),length(n4));
214
215   %%%% Binomial Grid %%%%
216   for ii = 1:1:length(n3)
217       n = n3(ii);
218
219       %%%% Binomial Grid for r,q,p and Discount Bond %%%%
220       [r_Option,q_Option,p_Option] = Binomial_Tree('r,q,p',n,t0,T,r0,sg,mu,kp);
221       [D_Bin_Option] = Binomial_Price(n,t0,T,r_Option,q_Option,p_Option,F,'Discount Bond');
222
223       %%%% Binomial Grid for Both European and American Options %%%%
224       cc = (T_Option-t0)./(T-t0).*n;
225       % ——— For 3.3.5 ——— %         ——> DB stands for Discount Bond <——
226       [Call_European_DB,Put_European_DB] = Binomial_Price(n,t0,T,r_Option,q_Option,p_Option,
              D_Bin_Option,...
227                                         'European Call and Put Discount Bond',cc,K);
228       % ——— For 3.4.2 ——— %
229       [Call_American_DB,Put_American_DB] = Binomial_Price(n,t0,T,r_Option,q_Option,p_Option,
              D_Bin_Option,...
230                                         'American Call and Put Discount Bond',cc,K);
231
232       %%%% Approximation Values %%%%
233       % ——— For 3.3.5 ——— %                              << ——— For 3.4.2 ——— >>
234       Call_European_DB_Graph(ii) = Call_European_DB(1,1); Call_American_DB_Graph(ii) =
              Call_American_DB(1,1);
235       Put_European_DB_Graph(ii) = Put_European_DB(1,1);    Put_American_DB_Graph(ii) =
              Put_American_DB(1,1);
236
237       %%%% Put-Call-Parity %%%%
238       % ——— For 3.3.5 ——— %
239       Call_Parity_DB_Graph(ii) = Put_European_DB(1,1)+Residual_Parity_DB;
240   end
241
242   %%%% Approximation Option Prices for r0 = 0.025 and n = 3020 %%%%
243   % ——— For 3.3.5 ——— %
244   Call_European_DB_Approx = Call_European_DB_Graph(length(n3));
245   Put_European_DB_Approx = Put_European_DB_Graph(length(n3));
246   %%%% Put-Call-Parity %%%%
247   Call_Parity_DB = Put_European_DB_Approx+Residual_Parity_DB;
248
249   % ——— For 3.4.2 ——— %
250   Call_American_DB_Approx = Call_American_DB_Graph(length(n3));
251   Put_American_DB_Approx = Put_American_DB_Graph(length(n3));
252
253   %%%% Approximation of Early Exercise Premiums as Functions of r0 =[0,...,1] %%%%
254   % ——— For 3.3.6 and 3.4.2 ——— %
255   for zz = 1:1:length(n4)
256       n = n4(zz);
257       for iii = 1:2
258       sg = sg_loop(iii);
259           for ii = 1:1:length(rr)
260               r0 = rr(ii);
261
262               %%%% Binomial Grid for r,q, p and Discount Bond %%%%
263               [r_Option,q_Option,p_Option] = Binomial_Tree('r,q,p',n,t0,T,r0,sg,mu,kp);
264               [D_Bin_Option] = Binomial_Price(n,t0,T,r_Option,q_Option,p_Option,F,'Discount Bond')
                      ;
265
266               %%%% Binomial Grid for Both European and American Options %%%%
267               % ——— For 3.3.5 and 3.3.6 ——— %
268               cc = (T_Option-t0)./(T-t0).*n;
269               [Call_European_DB,Put_European_DB] = Binomial_Price(n,t0,T,r_Option,q_Option,
                      p_Option,D_Bin_Option,'European Call and Put Discount Bond',cc,K);
270
271               % ——— For 3.4.2 ——— %
272               if sg == 0.04
```

21

```matlab
273             [Call_American_DB,Put_American_DB] = Binomial_Price(n,t0,T,r_Option,q_Option,
                    p_Option,D_Bin_Option,'American Call and Put Discount Bond',cc,K);
274
275             %%%% Approximation Values of Early Exercise Premium %%%%
276             Early_Exercise_Premium_Call_DB(1,ii) = Call_American_DB(1,1)-Call_European_DB(1,1);
277             Early_Exercise_Premium_Put_DB(1,ii) = Put_American_DB(1,1)-Put_European_DB(1,1);
278         end
279
280         % ----- For 3.3.6 ----- %
281         %%%% Approximation Values of Straddle Price %%%%
282         Straddle(iii,ii,zz) = Call_European_DB(1,1)+Put_European_DB(1,1);
283         %%%% Extra Analysis: Price Evolution DB, Call and Put on DB %%%%
284         D_Bin_Option_Graph1(iii,ii,zz) = D_Bin_Option(1,1);
285         Call_Europ_DB_Graph1(iii,ii,zz) = Call_European_DB(1,1);
286         Put_Europ_DB_Graph1(iii,ii,zz) = Put_European_DB(1,1);
287         end
288     end
289 end
290
291 % ----- For 3.3.6 ----- %
292 %%%% Approximation Value of Straddle for r0 = 0.025 %%%%
293 % For sigma = 0.04 %                              % For sigma = 0.071 %
294 Straddle_Approx_sg_low = Straddle(1,2,length(zz));       Straddle_Approx_sg_high = Straddle(2,2,
          length(zz));
295
296 %
    _____%

297 %%%% ----- Plotting ----- %%%%
298 %%%% Convergence of European Put and Call Price Approximation for increasing n %%%%
299 % ----- For 3.3.5 ----- %
300 kk = kk+1;
301 figure(kk)       % <<<< Figure 6 in Report >>>>
302 Options_Combined = [Call_European_DB_Graph;Put_European_DB_Graph];
303 plot(n3,Options_Combined,'LineWidth',1.5)
304 grid on
305 axis([0 inf 0 25])
306 title('European Call and Put Price','FontSize',14,'FontWeight','bold')
307 xlabel('Subperiod (n)','FontSize',12);
308 ylabel('Price','FontSize',12);
309 legend({'European Call Approximation','European Put Approximation'}...
310         ,'Location','east')
311 saveas(gcf,'3.3.5_European_CallPut.jpg');
312
313 % ----- For 3.4.2 ----- %
314 %%%% Convergence of Call and Put Price with increasing n %%%%
315 AmericanOptions_Combined = [Call_American_DB_Graph;Put_American_DB_Graph];
316 kk = kk+1;
317 figure(kk)       % <<<< Figure 9 in Report >>>>
318 plot(n3,AmericanOptions_Combined,'LineWidth',1.5)
319 axis([0 inf 22 inf])
320 title('American Call and Put Option on Coupon Bond','FontSize',14,'FontWeight','bold')
321 xlabel('Subperiods (n)','FontSize',12);
322 ylabel('Fair Value','FontSize',12);
323 legend({'American Call on DB','American Put on DB'}...
324         ,'Location','southeast')
325 saveas(gcf,'3.4.2_PriceConvergence_CallPut.jpg');
326
327 %%%% Early Exercise Premiums as Functions of r0 %%%%
328 % For Call %
329 kk = kk+1;
330 figure(kk)       % <<<< Figure 10(a) in Report >>>>
331 plot(rr,Early_Exercise_Premium_Call_DB,'k','LineWidth',1.5)
332 title('Early Exercise Premium Call Option Discount Bond','FontSize',14,'FontWeight','bold')
333 xlabel('Spot Interest Rate (r_0)','FontSize',12);
334 ylabel('Early Exercise Premium','FontSize',12);
335 saveas(gcf,'3.4.2_EarlyExercisePremium_Call.jpg');
336
337 % For Put %
338 kk = kk+1;
339 figure(kk)       % <<<< Figure 10(b) in Report >>>>
340 plot(rr,Early_Exercise_Premium_Put_DB,'k','LineWidth',1.5)
341 title('Early Exercise Premium of Put Option Discount Bond','FontSize',14,'FontWeight','bold')
342 xlabel('Spot Interest Rate (r_0)','FontSize',12);
343 ylabel('Early Exercise Premium','FontSize',12);
344 saveas(gcf,'3.4.2_EarlyExercisePremium_Put.jpg');
345
346 % ----- For 3.3.6 ----- %
347 %%%% Value of Straddle as a Function of r0 = [0,...,1] %%%%
348 for pp = 1:1:zz
349     kk = kk+1;
350         figure(kk)       % <<<< Figure 7 in Report >>>>
```

```
351    plot(rr,Straddle(:,:,pp),'LineWidth',1.5)
352    axis([0 1 10 45])
353    title('Fair Straddle Value','FontSize',14,'FontWeight','bold')
354    xlabel('Spot Interest Rate (r)','FontSize',12);
355    ylabel('Fair Value','FontSize',12);
356    legend({'Straddle Value for \sigma = 0.04','Straddle Value for \sigma = 0.071'}...
357            ,'Location','northeast')
358 end
359 % ----- Additional Analysis ----- %
360 kk = kk+1;
361 figure(kk)      % <<<< Figure 8(a) and (b) in Report >>>>
362 Options_Combined = [Put_Europ_DB_Graph1(:,:,length(zz));Call_Europ_DB_Graph1(:,:,length(zz))];
363 p2 = plot(rr,Options_Combined,'LineWidth',1.5);
364 set(p2,{'color'},num2cell([0,0.7,0;0,0,1;1,0,0;0,0,0],2));
365 title('European Put','FontSize',14);
366 xlabel('Interest Rate (r_0)','FontSize',12)
367 ylabel('Fair Value','FontSize',12)
368 legend({'European Put Price for \sigma=0.04','European Put Price for \sigma=0.071',...
369         'European Call Price for \sigma=0.04','European Call Price for \sigma=0.071'},'Location'
             ,'northeast')
370 % saveas(gcf,'3.3.6_CallPut_DB_Varying_r.jpg');
371
372 kk = kk+1;
373 figure(kk)      % <<<< Figure 8(c) and (d) in Report >>>>
374 plot(rr,D_Bin_Option_Graph1(:,:,length(zz)),'LineWidth',1.5)
375 title('Discount Bond','FontSize',14);
376 xlabel('Interest Rate (r_0)','FontSize',12)
377 ylabel('Fair Value','FontSize',12)
378 legend({'Discount Bond Price for \sigma=0.04','Discount Bond Price for \sigma=0.071'}...
379         ,'Location','southwest')
380 % saveas(gcf,'3.3.6_DB_Varying_r.jpg');
381
382 %% 3.4.1   << European Call and Put on a Coupon Bond >>
383 %% 3.4.3   << American Call and Put on a Coupon Bond >>
384 r0 = 0.025;                          % Redefining the initial Interest Rate
385 sg = 0.04;                           % Redefining the Interest Rate's Volatility
386 K_Coupon = 0.98*F_Coupon_Bond;       % Strike Price: Valid for all Options on a Coupon
         Bond
387
388 % ----- For Put-Call-Parity ----- %           --> Coupon Bond Value and Present Value of Coupon
          Payments <--
389 Residual_Parity_CB = B-D(t0,T_Option,r0,mu,sg,kp)*K_Coupon-D(t0,1,r0,mu,sg,kp)*Coupon...
390                     -D(t0,2,r0,mu,sg,kp)*Coupon-D(t0,2.5,r0,mu,sg,kp)*Coupon/2;
391
392 %%% Preallocation of Matrices %%%
393 % ----- For 3.4.1 ----- %
394 Call_European_CB_Graph = nan(1,length(n_Coupon));    Put_European_CB_Graph = nan(1,length(
         n_Coupon));
395 Call_Parity_CB_Graph = nan(1,length(n_Coupon));
396 % ----- For 3.4.3 ----- %
397 Call_American_CB_Graph = nan(1,length(n_Coupon));    Put_American_CB_Graph = nan(1,length(
         n_Coupon));
398 Early_Exercise_Premium_Call_CB = nan(1,length(rr));
399 Early_Exercise_Premium_Put_CB = nan(1,length(rr));
400
401 for ii = 1:1:length(n_Coupon)
402    n = n_Coupon(ii);
403
404    %%% Binomial Grid r, q, p and Coupon Bond %%%
405    [r_Coupon,q_Coupon,p_Coupon] = Binomial_Tree('r,q,p',n,t0,T_Coupon,r0,sg,mu,kp);
406    [D_Bin_Coupon] = Binomial_Price(n,t0,T_Coupon,r_Coupon,q_Coupon,p_Coupon,F_Coupon_Bond,'
         Coupon Bond',c);
407
408    cc = ((T_Option-t0)/(T_Coupon-t0))*n;    % Obtaining the Column-Number where the Option
         expires
409
410    %%% Approximation Option Prices %%%
411    [Call_European_CB,Put_European_CB] = Binomial_Price(n,t0,T_Coupon,r_Coupon,q_Coupon,p_Coupon
         ,D_Bin_Coupon...
412                             ,'European Call and Put Coupon Bond',cc,K_Coupon);
413    [Call_American_CB,Put_American_CB] = Binomial_Price(n,t0,T_Coupon,r_Coupon,q_Coupon,p_Coupon
         ,D_Bin_Coupon...
414                             ,'American Call and Put Coupon Bond',cc,K_Coupon);
415
416    %%% Approximation Values %%%
417    Call_European_CB_Graph(ii) = Call_European_CB(1,1); Put_European_CB_Graph(ii) =
         Put_European_CB(1,1);
418    Call_American_CB_Graph(ii) = Call_American_CB(1,1); Put_American_CB_Graph(ii) =
         Put_American_CB(1,1);
419
420    % ----- For 3.4.1 ----- %
421    %%% Put-Call-Parity %%%         --> CB stands for 'Coupon Bond' <--
```

```matlab
422        Call_Parity_CB_Graph(ii) = Put_European_CB(1,1)+Residual_Parity_CB;
423 end
424
425 %%% Approximation Values: Option on Coupon Bond %%%
426 % ---- For 3.4.1 ---- %
427 Call_European_CB_Approx = Call_European_CB_Graph(length(n_Coupon));
428 Put_European_CB_Approx = Put_European_CB_Graph(length(n_Coupon));
429
430 %%% Put-Call-Parity %%%            --> CB stands for 'Coupon Bond' <--
431 Call_Parity_CB = Put_European_CB_Approx+Residual_Parity_CB;
432 % ---- For 3.4.3 ---- %
433 Call_American_CB_Approx = Call_American_CB(1,1);
434 Put_American_CB_Approx = Put_American_CB(1,1);
435
436 % ---- For 3.4.3 ---- %
437 if n == n_Coupon(length(n_Coupon))
438     for iii = 1:1:length(rr)
439         r0 = rr(iii);
440
441         %%% Binomial Grid r, q, p and Coupon Bond %%%
442         [r_Coupon,q_Coupon,p_Coupon] = Binomial_Tree('r,q,p',n,t0,T_Coupon,r0,sg,mu,kp);
443         [D_Bin_Coupon] = Binomial_Price(n,t0,T_Coupon,r_Coupon,q_Coupon,p_Coupon,F_Coupon_Bond,'
                    Coupon Bond',c);
444
445         %%% Approximation Option Prices %%%
446         [Call_European_CB,Put_European_CB] = Binomial_Price(n,t0,T_Coupon,r_Coupon,q_Coupon,
                    p_Coupon,D_Bin_Coupon,'European Call and Put Coupon Bond',cc,K_Coupon);
447         [Call_American_CB,Put_American_CB] = Binomial_Price(n,t0,T_Coupon,r_Coupon,q_Coupon,
                    p_Coupon,D_Bin_Coupon,'American Call and Put Coupon Bond',cc,K_Coupon);
448
449         %%% Approximation Early Exercise Premiums as Functions of r0=[0,...,1] %%%
450         Early_Exercise_Premium_Call_CB(iii) = Call_American_CB(1,1)-Call_European_CB(1,1);
451         Early_Exercise_Premium_Put_CB(iii) = Put_American_CB(1,1)-Put_European_CB(1,1);
452     end
453 end
454 %
_____%

455 %%% ---- Plotting ---- %%%
456 % ---- For 3.4.3 ---- %
457 %%% Early Exercise Premiums as Functions of r0 %%%
458 % ---- For Call and Put ---- %
459 kk = kk+1;
460 figure(kk)        % <<<< Figure 11 in Report >>>>
461 plot(rr,Early_Exercise_Premium_Call_CB,'r','LineWidth',1.5)
462 hold on
463 plot(rr,Early_Exercise_Premium_Put_CB,'b','LineWidth',1.5)
464 title('Early Exercise Premium Call and Put Option on Coupon Bond','FontSize',14,'FontWeight','
            bold')
465 xlabel('Spot Interest Rate (r_0)','FontSize',12);
466 ylabel('Early Exercise Premium','FontSize',12);
467 legend({'Early Exercise Premium Call','Early Exercise Premium Put'},'Location','southeast')
468 saveas(gcf,'3.4.3_EarlyExercisePremium_PutCall.jpg');
469
470 disp('Computational Effort for Assignment 5 (without Effort for Command-Window displaying):')
471 toc
472
473 %% Displaying Results in Command Window %%
474 format long
475 % ---- For Task 3.2 ---- %       <<<< See also Table 2 in Report >>>>
476 disp('Task 3.2: Numerical Approximations and Exact Values for Expectation and Variance:')
477 Description = {'Numerical Approximation';'Exact Value';'Numerical Approximation';'Exact Value'};
478 Ten = [round(Er_Approx_Graph(1),4);round(Er_Exact,4);round(Var_Approx_Graph(1),9);round(
            Var_Exact,9)];
479 Twenty = [round(Er_Approx_Graph(2),4);round(Er_Exact,4);round(Var_Approx_Graph(2),9);round(
            Var_Exact,9)];
480 One_Hundred = [round(Er_Approx_Graph(3),4);round(Er_Exact,4);round(Var_Approx_Graph(3),9);round(
            Var_Exact,9)];
481 R1 = table(Description,Ten,Twenty,One_Hundred,...
482     'RowNames',{'(1.0) Expectation','(1.1)','(2.0) Variance','(2.1)'});
483 R1.Properties.VariableNames = {'Number_Subperiods','Ten','Twenty','One_Hundred'};
484 disp(R1)
485
486 % ---- For Task 3.3.1 and 3.3.2 ---- %
487 disp('Tasks 3.3.1 and 3.3.2: Approximation Values for increasing Number of Subperiods (n):')
488 Description = {'Discount Bond: Approximation';'Discount Bond: Exact Value';...
489         'Futures Contract: Approximation';'Futures Contract: Exact Value';...
490         'Forward Contract: Approximation';'Forward Contract: Exact Value'};
491 Twenty2 = [round(D_Bin_Graph(1),4);round(D_Exact,4);round(H_Bin_Graph(1),4);...
492         round(H_Exact,4);round(G_Bin_Graph(1),4);round(G_Exact,4)];
493 Thousand_Twenty = [round(D_Bin_Graph(11),4);round(D_Exact,4);round(H_Bin_Graph(11),4);...
494         round(H_Exact,4);round(G_Bin_Graph(11),4);round(G_Exact,4)];
```

```
495  ThreeThousand_Twenty = [round(D_Bin_Graph(31),4);round(D_Exact,4);round(H_Bin_Graph(31),4);...
496                          round(H_Exact,4);round(G_Bin_Graph(31),4);round(G_Exact,4)];
497  R2 = table(Description,Twenty2,Thousand_Twenty,ThreeThousand_Twenty,...
498       'RowNames',{'(3.0) Task 3.3.1','(3.1)','(4.0) Task 3.3.2','(4.1)','(4.2)','(4.3)'});
499  R2.Properties.VariableNames = {'Number_Subperiods','Twenty','Thousand_Twenty','
         ThreeThousand_Twenty'};
500  disp(R2)
501  %%
502  disp('Task 3.3.3: Fair Value Coupon Bond for r = r0 over remaining Time to Maturity:')
503  Description = {'Coupon Bond Price'};
504  Zero_Years = round(B_Exact(1),4);
505  Six_Years = round(B_Exact(61),4);
506  Twelve_Years = round(B_Exact(length(t)),4);
507  R3 = table(Description,Twelve_Years,Six_Years,Zero_Years,'RowNames',{'(5.0) Task 3.3.3'});
508  % R3.Properties.VariableNames = {'Time_to_Maturity','Twelve_years','6_years','0_years'};
509  disp(R3)
510  % ----- For Task 3.3.4 ----- %
511  disp('Task 3.3.4: Futures Contract on a Coupon Bond Value Approximation:')
512  Description = {'Futures Contract: Approximation'};
513  R4 = table(Description,round(H_CouponBond_Bin(1,1),4),'RowNames',{'(6.0) Task 3.3.4'});
514  R4.Properties.VariableNames = {'Number_Subperiods','ThreeThousand_SixHundred'};
515  disp(R4)
516  % ----- For Tasks 3.3.5 and 3.4.2 ----- %      <<<< See also Table 3 in Report >>>>
517  disp('Tasks 3.3.5 and 3.4.2: Approximation Values for Increasing Subperiods (n)')
518  Description = {'European Call on Discount Bond';'Put-Call-Parity: Call';'European Put on
         Discount Bond';...
519                'American Call on Discount Bond';'American Put on Discount Bond'};
520  Twenty3 = [round(Call_European_DB_Graph(1),4);round(Call_Parity_DB_Graph(1),4);round(
         Put_European_DB_Graph(1),4);...
521             round(Call_American_DB_Graph(1),4);round(Put_American_DB_Graph(1),4)];
522  Hundred_Twenty = [round(Call_European_DB_Graph(2),4);round(Call_Parity_DB_Graph(2),4);round(
         Put_European_DB_Graph(2),4);...
523             round(Call_American_DB_Graph(2),4);round(Put_American_DB_Graph(2),4)];
524  Thousand_Twenty = [round(Call_European_DB_Graph(11),4);round(Call_Parity_DB_Graph(11),4);round(
         Put_European_DB_Graph(11),4);...
525             round(Call_American_DB_Graph(11),4);round(Put_American_DB_Graph(11),4)];
526  R5 = table(Description,Twenty3,Hundred_Twenty,Thousand_Twenty,...
527       'RowNames',{'(7.0) Task 3.3.5','(7.1)','(7.2)','(8.0) Task 3.4.2','(8.1)'});
528  R5.Properties.VariableNames = {'Number_Subperiods','Twenty','Hundred_Twenty','Thousand_Twenty'};
529  disp(R5)
530  % ----- For Task 3.3.6 ----- %          <<<< See also Table 4 in Report >>>>
531  disp('Task 3.3.6: Straddle on Discount Bond Value Approximation for sigma = [0.04,0.071] and n =
         1020:')
532  Sigma = [0.04;0.04;0.04;0.071;0.071;0.071];
533  Interest_Rate = [0.025;0.25;0.7;0.025;0.25;0.7];
534  Price_Approximation = [round(Straddle(1,2,2),4);round(Straddle(1,11,2),4);round(Straddle(1,29,2)
         ,4);...
535                         round(Straddle(2,2,2),4);round(Straddle(2,11,2),4);round(Straddle(2,29,2)
         ,4)];
536  R6 = table(Sigma,Interest_Rate,Price_Approximation);
537  disp(R6)
538  % ----- For Tasks 3.4.1 and 3.4.3 ----- %
539  disp('Tasks 3.4.1 and 3.4.3: Approximation Values for Increasing Subperiods (n)')
540  Description = {'European Call on Coupon Bond';'European Put on Coupon Bond';...
541                'American Call on Coupon Bond';'American Put on Coupon Bond'};
542  Hundred_Twenty = [round(Call_European_CB_Graph(1),4);round(Put_European_CB_Graph(1),4);...
543             round(Call_American_CB_Graph(1),4);round(Put_American_CB_Graph(1),4)];
544  Thousand_TwoHundred = [round(Call_European_CB_Graph(3),4);round(Put_European_CB_Graph(3),4);...
545             round(Call_American_CB_Graph(3),4);round(Put_American_CB_Graph(3),4)];
546  ThreeThousand_SixHundred = [round(Call_European_CB_Graph(4),4);round(Put_European_CB_Graph(4),4)
         ;...
547                         round(Call_American_CB_Graph(4),4);round(Put_American_CB_Graph(4),4)
         ];
548  R7 = table(Description,Hundred_Twenty,Thousand_TwoHundred,ThreeThousand_SixHundred,...
549            'RowNames',{'(9.0) Task 3.4.1','(9.1)','(10.0) Task 3.4.3','(10.1)'});
550  R7.Properties.VariableNames = {'Number_Subperiods','Hundred_Twenty','Thousand_TwoHundred',...
551                                'ThreeThousand_SixHundred'};
552  disp(R7)
553
554  disp('Overall Computational Effort for Assignment 5:')
555  toc
```

Binomial_Tree.m

```
1  function [r,q,p,w] = Binomial_Tree(Mode,n,t0,T,r0,sg,mu,kp)
2
3  dt=(T-t0)./n;                        % dt represents 'Delta*t'
4  dr=sg.*sqrt(dt);
```

```
 5
 6  if strcmp(Mode,'r,q,p')
 7
 8      %%%% Preallocation of Matrices %%%%
 9      r=zeros(n+1,n+1);              % r = spot interest rate
10      q=zeros(n+1,n+1);              % q = transition probability of an upward move
11      p=zeros(n+1,n+1);              % p = transition probability of an downward move
12
13      %%%% Binomial Grid of r, q and p %%%%
14      for j=1:1:n+1
15          for k=1:1:j
16              r(j,k)= r0+(k-1).*dr-(j-k).*dr;
17              q(j,k)=0.5+0.5.*kp.*(mu-r(j,k)).*sqrt(dt)./sg;
18              q(j,k)=max(0,min(1,q(j,k))); % censoring q and p to I=[0,...,1]
19              p(j,k)=1-q(j,k);
20          end
21      end
22
23  elseif strcmp(Mode,'r,q,p,w')
24
25      %%%% Preallocation of Matrices %%%%
26      r=zeros(n+1,n+1);              % r = spot interest rate
27      q=zeros(n+1,n+1);              % q = transition probability of an upward move
28      p=zeros(n+1,n+1);              % p = transition probability of an downward move
29      w=zeros(n+1,n+1);              % w = total probability
30      w(1,1)=1;
31
32      %%%% Binomial Grid of r, q, p and w %%%%
33      for j=1:1:n+1
34          for k=1:1:j
35              r(j,k)= r0+(k-1).*dr-(j-k).*dr;
36              q(j,k)=0.5+0.5.*kp.*(mu-r(j,k)).*sqrt(dt)./sg;
37              q(j,k)=max(0,min(1,q(j,k))); % censoring q to [-1,...,1]
38              p(j,k)=1-q(j,k);
39
40              if j>1
41                  if k==1
42                      w(j,k)= w(j-1,k).*p(j-1,k); % account for down-moves only
43                  elseif k==j % when we are on the diagonal
44                      w(j,k)= w(j-1,k-1).*q(j-1,k-1); % account for up-moves only
45                  else
46                      w(j,k)= w(j-1,k).*p(j-1,k)+w(j-1,k-1).*q(j-1,k-1); % account for both up-
                          and down-moves
47                  end
48              end
49          end
50      end
51  else
52      disp('Please type in either 'r,q,p' or 'r,q,p,w' as the first Input-Variable.')
53      r = 'Wrong Input-Variables';
54      q = 'Wrong Input-Variables';
55      p = 'Wrong Input-Variables';
56      w = 'Wrong Input-Variables';
57  end
```

Binomial_Price.m

```
 1  function [Bin1,Bin2] = Binomial_Price(n,t0,T,r,q,p,F,Type,cc,ccc)
 2
 3  dt = (T-t0)./n;                    % dt represents 'Delta*t'
 4
 5  if nargin < 9
 6
 7      %%%% ----- Discount Bond ----- %%%%
 8      if strcmp(Type,'Discount Bond')
 9
10      %%%% Preallocation of Matrices %%%%
11      D_Bin = zeros(n+1,n+1);
12      D_Bin(n+1,:) = ones(n+1,1)*F;       % The Terminal Value of the Binomial Tree is the Face
                Value F
13
14      %%%% Binomial Grid %%%%
15      for j = n:-1:1
16          for k = 1:1:j
17              D_Bin(j,k) = exp(-r(j,k)*dt)*(D_Bin(j+1,k+1)*q(j,k)+D_Bin(j+1,k)*p(j,k));
18          end
19      end
20      end
```

```matlab
21          Bin1 = D_Bin;
22      elseif nargin == 9
23
24          %%% ----- Futures Contract on Discount Bond ----- %%%
25          if strcmp(Type,'Futures Contract Discount Bond')
26
27              %%% Preallocation of Matrices %%%
28              D_Bin = zeros(n+1,n+1);
29              D_Bin(n+1,:) = ones(n+1,1)*F;        % The Terminal Value of the Binomial Tree is the Face
                    Value F
30
31              %%% Binomial Grid %%%
32              for j = n:-1:1
33                  for k = 1:1:j
34                      D_Bin(j,k) = exp(-r(j,k)*dt)*(D_Bin(j+1,k+1)*q(j,k)+D_Bin(j+1,k)*p(j,k));
35                  end
36              end
37
38              %%% Preallocation of Matrices %%%
39              H_Bin = zeros(n+1,n+1);
40              H_Bin(cc+1,:) = D_Bin(cc+1,:);
41
42              %%% Binomial Grid %%%
43              for j = cc:-1:1
44                  for k = 1:1:cc
45                      H_Bin(j,k) = H_Bin(j+1,k+1)*q(j,k)+H_Bin(j+1,k)*p(j,k);
46                  end
47              end
48
49              Bin1 = D_Bin;
50              Bin2 = H_Bin;
51
52          %%% ----- Coupon Bond ----- %%%
53          elseif strcmp(Type,'Coupon Bond')
54              c = cc;
55
56              %%% Preallocation of Matrices %%%
57              D_Bin = zeros(n+1,n+1);
58              D_Bin(n+1,:) = ones(n+1,1)*F*(1+c);
59
60              %%% Binomial Grid %%%
61              for j=n:-1:1
62                  for k=1:1:j
63                      % Checking whether Coupon-Payment is due
64                      if mod(j,(n/T)) == 1 && j > 1
65                          D_Bin(j,k)=(F.*c)+exp(-r(j,k)*dt)*(D_Bin(j+1,k+1)*q(j,k)+D_Bin(j+1,k)*p(j,k)
                                );
66                      else
67                          D_Bin(j,k)=exp(-r(j,k)*dt)*(D_Bin(j+1,k+1)*q(j,k)+D_Bin(j+1,k)*p(j,k));
68                      end
69                  end
70              end
71              Bin1 = D_Bin;
72          end
73
74      elseif nargin == 10
75
76          %%% ----- Futures Contract on Coupon Bond ----- %%%
77          if strcmp(Type,'Futures Contract Coupon Bond')
78              c = cc;
79              cc = ccc;
80
81              %%% Preallocation of Matrices %%%
82              D_Bin = zeros(n+1,n+1);
83              D_Bin(n+1,:) = ones(n+1,1)*F*(1+c);
84
85              %%% Binomial Grid %%%
86              for j=n:-1:1
87                  for k=1:1:j
88                      % Checking whether Coupon-Payment is due
89                      if mod(j,(n/T)) == 1 && j > 1
90                          D_Bin(j,k)=(F.*c)+exp(-r(j,k)*dt)*(D_Bin(j+1,k+1)*q(j,k)+D_Bin(j+1,k)*p(j,k)
                                );
91                      else
92                          D_Bin(j,k)=exp(-r(j,k)*dt)*(D_Bin(j+1,k+1)*q(j,k)+D_Bin(j+1,k)*p(j,k));
93                      end
94                  end
95              end
96
97              %%% Preallocation of Matrices %%%
98              H_Bin = zeros(n+1,n+1);
99              H_Bin(cc+1,:) = D_Bin(cc+1,:);
```

```
100
101         %%% Binomial Grid %%%
102         for j=cc:-1:1
103             for k=1:1:cc
104                 H_Bin(j,k) = H_Bin(j+1,k+1)*q(j,k)+H_Bin(j+1,k)*p(j,k);
105             end
106         end
107         Bin1 = H_Bin;
108
109     %%% ----- European Call and Put on Discount Bond ----- %%%
110     elseif strcmp(Type,'European Call and Put Discount Bond')
111         D_Bin = F;
112         K = ccc;
113
114         %%% Preallocation of Matrices %%%
115         Call_Bin = zeros(cc+1,n+1);
116         Put_Bin = zeros(cc+1,n+1);
117
118         %%% Predetermination of Terminal Values %%%
119         Call_Bin(cc+1,:) = max(D_Bin(cc+1,:)-K,0);
120         Put_Bin(cc+1,:) = max(K-D_Bin(cc+1,:),0);
121
122         %%% Binomial Grid %%%
123         for j = cc:-1:1
124             for k = 1:1:cc
125                 Call_Bin(j,k) = exp(-r(j,k)*dt)*(Call_Bin(j+1,k+1)*q(j,k)...
126                                 +Call_Bin(j+1,k)*p(j,k));
127                 Put_Bin(j,k) = exp(-r(j,k)*dt)*(Put_Bin(j+1,k+1)*q(j,k)...
128                                 +Put_Bin(j+1,k)*p(j,k));
129             end
130         end
131         Bin1 = Call_Bin;
132         Bin2 = Put_Bin;
133
134     %%% ----- European Call and Put on Coupon Bond ----- %%%
135     elseif strcmp(Type,'European Call and Put Coupon Bond')
136         D_Bin = F;
137         K = ccc;
138
139         %%% Preallocation of Matrices %%%
140         Call_Bin = zeros(n+1,n+1);
141         Put_Bin = zeros(n+1,n+1);
142
143         %%% Predetermination of Terminal Values %%%
144         Call_Bin(cc+1,:) = max(D_Bin(cc+1,:)-K,0);
145         Put_Bin(cc+1,:) = max(K-D_Bin(cc+1,:),0);
146
147         %%% Binomial Grid %%%
148         for j=cc:-1:1
149             for k=1:1:cc
150                 Call_Bin(j,k) = exp(-r(1,1)*dt)*(Call_Bin(j+1,k+1)*q(j,k)+Call_Bin(j+1,k)*p(j,k)
                    );
151                 Put_Bin(j,k) = exp(-r(1,1)*dt)*(Put_Bin(j+1,k+1)*q(j,k)+Put_Bin(j+1,k)*p(j,k));
152             end
153         end
154         Bin1 = Call_Bin;
155         Bin2 = Put_Bin;
156
157     %%% ----- American Call and Put on Discount Bond ----- %%%
158     elseif strcmp(Type,'American Call and Put Discount Bond')
159         D_Bin = F;
160         K = ccc;
161
162         %%% Preallocation of Matrices %%%
163         Call_Bin = zeros(cc+1,n+1);
164         Put_Bin = zeros(cc+1,n+1);
165
166         %%% Predetermination of Terminal Values %%%
167         Call_Bin(cc+1,:) = max(D_Bin(cc+1,:)-K,0);
168         Put_Bin(cc+1,:) = max(K-D_Bin(cc+1,:),0);
169
170         %%% Binomial Grid %%%
171         for j = cc:-1:1
172             for k = 1:1:cc
173                 Call_Bin(j,k) = max(exp(-r(j,k)*dt)*(Call_Bin(j+1,k+1)*q(j,k)+...
174                                 Call_Bin(j+1,k)*p(j,k)),D_Bin(j,k)-K);
175                 Put_Bin(j,k) = max(exp(-r(j,k)*dt)*(Put_Bin(j+1,k+1)*q(j,k)+...
176                                 Put_Bin(j+1,k)*p(j,k)),K-D_Bin(j,k));
177             end
178         end
179         Bin1 = Call_Bin;
180         Bin2 = Put_Bin;
```

```matlab
181
182        %%% ---- American Call and Put on Coupon Bond ---- %%%
183        elseif strcmp(Type,'American Call and Put Coupon Bond')
184            D_Bin = F;
185            K = ccc;
186
187            %%% Preallocation of Matrices %%%
188            Call_Bin = zeros(n+1,n+1);
189            Put_Bin = zeros(n+1,n+1);
190
191            %%% Predetermination of Terminal Values %%%
192            Call_Bin(cc+1,:) = max(D_Bin(cc+1,:)-K,0);
193            Put_Bin(cc+1,:) = max(K-D_Bin(cc+1,:),0);
194
195            %%% Binomial Grid %%%
196            for j=cc:-1:1
197                for k=1:1:cc
198                    Call_Bin(j,k) = max(exp(-r(1,1)*dt)*(Call_Bin(j+1,k+1)*q(j,k)...
199                                    +Call_Bin(j+1,k)*p(j,k)),D_Bin(j,k)-K);
200                    Put_Bin(j,k) = max(exp(-r(1,1)*dt)*(Put_Bin(j+1,k+1)*q(j,k)...
201                                    +Put_Bin(j+1,k)*p(j,k)),K-D_Bin(j,k));
202                end
203            end
204
205            Bin1 = Call_Bin;
206            Bin2 = Put_Bin;
207        end
208    else
209        disp('Wrong Input. For Price Approximation of a Discount Bond: "Discount Bond".')
210        disp('For a Futures Contract on a Discount Bond: "Futures Contract Discount Bond".')
211        disp('For a Coupon Bond: "Coupon Bond".')
212        disp('For a Futures Contract on a Coupon Bond: "Futures Contract Coupon Bond".')
213        disp('For a European Call and/ or Put Option on a Discount Bond: "European Call and Put
             Discount Bond".')
214        disp('For a European Call and/ or Put Option on a Coupon Bond: "European Call and Put Coupon
             Bond".')
215        disp('For an American Call and/ or Put Option on a Discount Bond: "American Call and Put
             Discount Bond".')
216        disp('For an American Call and/ or Put Option on a Coupon Bond: "American Call and Put
             Coupon Bond".')
217    end
218 end
```

References

Ritchken, P. (1996), *Derivative Markets - Theory, Strategy, and Application*, part six edn, HarperCollins College Publishers.

Vasicek, O. (1977), 'An equilibrium characterization of the term structure', *Journal of Financial Economics* **5**(2), 177 – 188.
    URL: *http://www.sciencedirect.com/science/article/pii/0304405X77900162*